XTREME PETS
SPIDERS

BY S.L. HAMILTON

Visit us at
www.abdopublishing.com

Published by ABDO Publishing Company, PO Box 398166, Minneapolis, MN 55439.
Copyright ©2014 by Abdo Consulting Group, Inc. International copyrights reserved in all
countries. No part of this book may be reproduced in any form without written permission
from the publisher. A&D Xtreme™ is a trademark and logo of ABDO Publishing Company.

Printed in the United States of America, North Mankato, Minnesota.
032013
092013

Editor: John Hamilton
Graphic Design: Sue Hamilton
Cover Design: Sue Hamilton
Cover Photo: Thinkstock
Interior Photos: AP-pgs 6-7; Corbis-pgs 8-9, 20 & 30-31; Getty Images-pgs 4-5, 12-13, 16-
17, 18, 19, 21, 24-25 & 26-27; Michael Leach-pgs 10-11; Glow Images-pgs 14 & 22-23;
Thinkstock-pgs 1, 2-3, 15, 28-29 & 32.

ABDO Booklinks
Web sites about Xtreme Pets are featured on our Book Links pages. These links are routinely
monitored and updated to provide the most current information available.
Web site: www.abdopublishing.com

Library of Congress Control Number: 2013931679

Cataloging-in-Publication Data

Hamilton, Sue.
 Spiders / Sue Hamilton.
   p. cm. -- (Xtreme pets)
 ISBN 978-1-61783-975-7
 1. Spiders--Juvenile literature. 2. Pets--Juvenile literature.   I. Title.
 595.4--dc23

                                              2013931679

CONTENTS

XTREME PETS: SPIDERS

There are more than 40,000 species of spiders. These eight-legged creatures live in trees, grass, underground burrows, water, and in homes. Many spiders make interesting pets. They are quiet and need little care. They molt their exoskeletons as they grow. Their unique food-catching abilities are fascinating to watch.

XTREME FACT– Some highly-venomous spiders, such as black widows, are illegal to own.

TARANTULAS

Tarantulas are the biggest spiders. They are also the most popular spider pets. The largest are Goliath bird-eater tarantulas. Their leg spans may reach 12 inches (30 cm). They live about 15-25 years. Bird-eaters eat live prey. They may eat birds as their name implies, but they are more likely to eat crickets, cockroaches, mice, and frogs.

XTREME FACT – Tarantulas have fangs and a venomous bite, but they usually only bite when threatened.

*Goliath Bird-eater
Tarantula*

The Mexican redknee tarantula is one of the most popular pet spiders. Mexican redknees are calm and have a less-harmful venom than other tarantulas. They grow to about 6 inches (15 cm). They molt, or shed their exoskeleton, as they grow. Redknees eat crickets and other large insects, small lizards, and mice. They live in burrows, and may live up to 30 years.

XTREME FACT– When threatened, tarantulas may flick bristly hairs off their bodies toward an attacker. These "urticating hairs" may cause a human to develop a rash. If hairs get caught in the eye, it is necessary to try to wash them out with water and see a doctor immediately.

Mexican
Redknee
Tarantula

Curlyhair tarantulas are calm spiders and popular pets. Curlyhairs may live up to 15 years. They grow to reach leg spans of 5.5 inches (14 cm).

The long hairs on their bodies and legs are used to detect vibrations made by their favorite foods: crickets, large insects, small lizards, and mice.

Curlyhair Tarantula

XTREME FACT – Curlyhair tarantulas are also called woolly tarantulas.

11

The Chilean rose hair tarantula, or "Rosie," is a favorite pet spider. It is often considered the least likely to bite. However, it can be nervous and may attack with urticating hairs. It may grow up to 5 inches (13 cm) long. It eats crickets, locusts, meal worms, houseflies, and cockroaches. They may live up to 20 years.

XTREME FACT – Rosies are very delicate after molting, or breaking out of their old exoskeletons. They should not be fed until their new "skin" has hardened. Their prey may hurt them!

*Chilean
Rose Hair
Tarantula*

WOLF SPIDERS

Wolf spiders grow to about 1 inch (2.5 cm) long. They do not make webs. They catch their food by hunting live prey. They have excellent eyesight, and can even see at night. Their superior sense of touch lets them "feel" vibrations made from prey. Wolf spiders eat houseflies, crickets, worms, and grasshoppers. They are calm pets and fascinating to watch hunt at night.

Wolf spiders have eight eyes: Two on top (only the left one is shown here), two large eyes in the middle, and four small eyes on the bottom.

TRAPDOOR SPIDERS

Trapdoor spiders are bold hunters with a unique method for capturing their prey. They build a tunnel-like burrow covered with a "trapdoor."

Trapdoor spiders grow up to 2.5 inches (6 cm) in length. While very interesting hunters, trapdoor spiders are not good pets. They are aggressive and will bite. Females live for up to 20 years. They spend nearly all of their time inside their burrows. Males live for 2-3 years, then leave their burrows to find mates. After reproducing, males die.

The trapdoor is made of soil, vegetation, and the spider's silk. The trapdoor is hinged by silk on one side.

When prey comes near the hatch, the spider flips open its trapdoor. The spider grabs its surprised prey and drags it into the burrow.

Jumping spiders are everywhere. There are more than 5,000 species worldwide. They are easily caught in backyards and windows by gently directing them into a container. Although small, often less than ½ inch (1.3 cm) long, they make good spider pets. They live for about one year.

XTREME FACT – Besides being able to leap, jumping spiders can run sideways and backwards.

Jumping spiders need a terrarium large enough for them to run and jump. They are interesting to watch hunt. They study, stalk, and leap onto their prey. Their unique eye patterns help them hunt. They have four eyes in front and four in back. Two of their front eyes are larger, which helps them track their prey. They eat houseflies, crickets, and other small insects.

Before leaping, jumping spiders anchor themselves to a solid surface with a silk line.

If their jump falls short, they have a safety line
that will keep them from falling.

XTREME FACT – Jumping spiders
may leap 50 times their body length!

FISHING SPIDERS

Fishing spiders live near water. They have hairs around their body that repel water. This allows them to float on a lake or pond as they wait for their food, which includes minnows, tadpoles, small frogs, and bugs.

Fishing spiders range in size from 1.5-3 inches (3.8-7.6 cm) long. They live for about one year. They need to be kept in a tank with shallow water and a dry area of rocks or branches that closely matches their natural habitat. While interesting to watch, they are aggressive and do not like to be handled.

XTREME FACT – Fishing spiders are also called raft spiders, dock spiders, and wharf spiders.

The same hairs that allow fishing spiders to float also detect movement and help them judge the size and location of their prey.

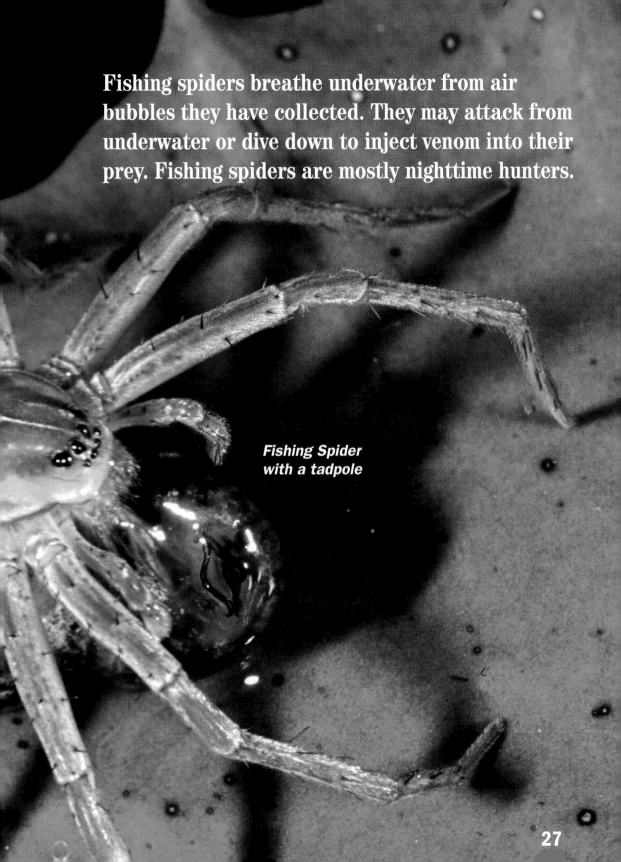

Fishing spiders breathe underwater from air bubbles they have collected. They may attack from underwater or dive down to inject venom into their prey. Fishing spiders are mostly nighttime hunters.

Fishing Spider with a tadpole

GRASS SPIDERS

Grass spiders live in many yards, making them easy spiders to collect as pets. Their sheet webs are often spun on the tops of blades of grass or near shrubs or other vegetation. These webs are easy to see in the morning when dew is on the ground.

Grass Spider with its prey

Grass spiders live from one to four years. Although they are only about 1-3 inches (2.5-7.6 cm) in size, pet grass spiders need large containers so they can construct their webs. One corner of their sheet web has a funnel-like shelter. The web is not super sticky. When a bug crawls or lands onto the web, grass spiders move quickly. They grab their insect prey and inject a paralyzing venom.

XTREME FACT – Birds sometimes steal grass spiders' webs because the soft silk makes a comfortable bed for their eggs.

GLOSSARY

AGGRESSIVE
Likely to attack with, or without, a reason to do so.

BURROW
An underground home. Some spiders live in burrows.

EXOSKELETON
The hard outside surface that frames a spider's body.

MOLT
For a spider, shedding its exoskeleton in order to grow bigger. Many spiders molt several times before reaching adulthood.

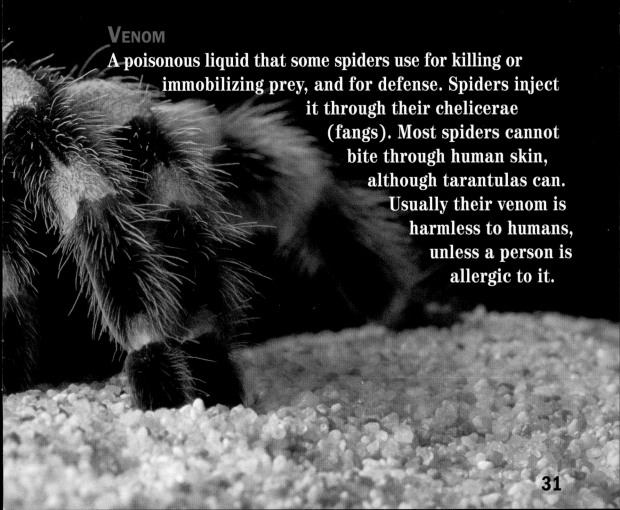

SILK

A thin, strong, and often sticky protein thread created by a spider and ejected from its body through spinneret glands. Spiders may use silk to create webs, nests, safety lines, and even "balloons" to move them through the air. They also may wrap up their prey with silk.

URTICATING HAIRS

In tarantulas, sharp bristly hairs that form on the spider's abdomen (belly) after several molts. A tarantula uses its back legs to flick the hairs at predators, aiming for the threat's eyes. The hairs cause irritation in skin, and may cause temporary blindness.

VENOM

A poisonous liquid that some spiders use for killing or immobilizing prey, and for defense. Spiders inject it through their chelicerae (fangs). Most spiders cannot bite through human skin, although tarantulas can. Usually their venom is harmless to humans, unless a person is allergic to it.

INDEX